Writing the Killer Mystery

Volume Two

Captivating Characters

A Guide to Creating the Players in Your Mystery Novel

by

Ron D. Voigts

Ron D. Voigts

Writing the Killer Mystery, Captivating Characters

All material and information in this book are considered factual and accurate to the author's and publisher's knowledge.

Paperback edition: September 2018, Night Wings Publishing

ISBN: 978-1719978408

Ron D. Voigts

Dedication

To my wife, Lois,

who has stuck with me and understood me

even when nobody else does

Ron D. Voigts

Books by Ron D. Voigts

Self-Published

Penelope and The Birthday Curse

Penelope and The Ghost's Treasure

Penelope and The Movie Star

Penelope and The Christmas Spirit

Claws of the Griffin

Night Wings Publishing

Strigoi, The Blood Bond

Champagne Book Group

The Witch's Daughter

The Fortune Teller's Secret

Writing the Killer Mystery

Volume One, Great Beginnings

Volume Two, Captivating Characters

Volume Three, Plotting the Murder

Ron D. Voigts

TABLE OF CONTENTS

Chapter One:
Some Front End Stuff

First things first, I don't like reading forwards, prologues, and front end matter. Get me to the good stuff. However, I have a philosophy behind this book, the series, in fact. So stop back later if you wish to jump ahead.

I planned a five-volume series on Writing the Killer Mystery with some goals.

- Ideally, from beginning to end, these five volumes should give an excellent working knowledge of writing a mystery. Articles appear under broader headings and can be read in series-order to gain better insight into an aspect of mystery writing.

- The series is not just to inform but to inspire. Need help in finding a motive, examine the list in that section. Trying to come up with something on your sleuth's background, a list of ideas is available for your perusal. If you're stumped how to create a supervillain, a list exists for that too. Remember, these suggestions are the beginnings to stimulate your imagination. You are the author of your mystery.

- I have another philosophy. My time to read, write, handle social media, keep up with current events, take time for entertainment, and have a social life pretty much keeps me busy from dawn to bedtime, so finding moments to get absorbed in a book are hard. So, I wrote this volume in bite-size chunks to be read in short sittings. Key points, bullets, numberings, and lists are used where possible to make things easier. Examples happen at the end of many sections if more understanding is needed. The whole point is to get information fast and easy.

- The articles can stand-alone too. If you are struggling to name your sleuth, stop by that section in Volume Two for inspiration. Read the article on guns in Volume Four if you need some background. By the way, I wrote this for writers. If you check out the gun section to learn how to field strip a Glock and reassemble it, you are looking in the wrong place. Articles for nearly every facet of mystery writing can be found in the five volumes.

Following is a brief outline of the characters included. Also, beginning in this volume, the focus will be on the killer rather than the perpetrator as noted in Volume One.

- The Sleuth

- The Victim

- The Killer

- The Suspects

- Special characters

- The Rest of the Cast

The ultimate goal in Volume Two is to create tools for creating Captivating Characters in the mystery novel.

Chapter Two:
The Sleuth

Professional or Amateur

Sleuths come in two types: amateurs and professionals. Arguably, some exist somewhere in between, but ultimately the division will be based on if they work within the legal system or outside it, perhaps looking in. And of course, professionals expect payment for their work while the amateurs do it out of the goodness of their hearts.

Some Professionals
Coroner
Crime Scene Investigator
Detective
Detective Inspector (British)
Lawyer
Medical Examiner
Military Investigator
Police Officer
Private Eye

Some Amateurs
Baker
Butcher
Doctor
Newspaper reporter
Nurse
Retired person
Spy
Teacher
Tinker
Basically, everyone not a professional

Once you determine which side of the fence your guy is on, you need to get to know him better.

On the professional side, you'll need to know how the sleuth operates. Understanding the law and how it works, especially in his neck of the woods, is essential. Of course, your crime solver could be a sheriff in some obscure little town and writes his own laws. But then again he may be a homicide detective in a major metropolitan area where understanding legality and how local police work happens is essential.

The amateur sleuth is less restricted concerning legal matter. Some basic stuff is still needed. Understanding laws and their implementation can be necessary. Ultimately this type of detective has a bit more freedom. Yet understanding her profession is required. If she is a news reporter, then she will be doing stuff reporters do. A retired gal once had a job and may still have interests in it, while being a member of the garden club and working part-time at the local hardware store. Sleuthing doctors still see patients when not solving crimes.

An excellent example of "know thy sleuth" mindset is Mike Connelly, who writes a series about Detective Harry Bosch. Connelly knows the workings of the LAPD inside and out. This kind of knowledge comes from doing a ride-along with the local police, having friends on the inside, and asking a lot of questions. All this gives his books an authentic feel.

Name, A Rose is a Rose or Something Like That

The Bard, aka Shakespeare, said, "What's in a name? That which we call a rose by any other name would smell as sweet." And yet call the fragrant flower *a dead fish* would not be the same.

Finding the right name for your sleuth can be exasperating. With a great name and some good writing, your guy or gal will be up there in the annals of famous detectives. Get it wrong, and he or she becomes another obscure name, forgotten. Plus a catchy name helps to propel book sales.

Later, I present a list of 50 detective names from books, TV, and movies. Some trends exist here. Some sleuths in fictional history become more memorable than others. Here are ten things to consider when naming your sleuth.

1. A name with a nice sound or ring. Rolls off the tongue. (Jim Rockford, Charlie Chan, Philip Marlowe)

2. A name identifiable with things we know, touch, or see. (Sam Spade, Richard Diamond, Thomas Magnum, John Shaft)

3. An uncommon first name with a common last name. (Phryne Fisher, Elijah Baley)

4. A typical first name with unique last name. (Dave Robicheaux, Harry Bosch)

5. An unusual first and last name. (Sherlock Holmes, Hercule Poirot, Ellery Queen, Nero Wolfe)

6. One name detectives. (Columbo, Cadfael, Lovejoy)

7. Names with titles. (Father Brown, Inspector Morse, Lord Peter Wimsey)

8. Alliteration of first and last names. (Charlie Chan, Shawn Spencer, Boston Blackie)

9. More nickname than a name. (Boston Blackie, Bulldog Drummond)

10. Initials with the last name. (V.I. Warshawski, Dr. R. Quincy M.E., C. Auguste Dupin)

So how do you come up with a good name? Listen to the sound. Do you like it? Is it catchy? Does it say detective or sleuth?

Remember this is the name you'll need to use throughout the entire book and maybe a series, so you better like it.

Fictional Detective Names
Sherlock Holmes
Richard Diamond
Harry Bosch
Sam Spade
Philip Marlowe
Hercule Poirot
Miss Jane Marple
Adrian Monk
Inspector Clouseau
Nancy Drew
Charlie Chan
Thomas Magnum
Columbo
Jessica Fletcher
Veronica Mars
Dave Robicheaux
Dick Tracy
Father Brown
Jim Rockford
John Shaft
Phryne Fisher
Bulldog Drummond
Ellery Queen
C. Auguste Dupin
Alex Cross
Lord Peter Wimsey
Precious Ramotswe
Ralph Dibny
Dirk Gently
V.I. Warshawski
Dr. Temperance "Bones" Brennan
Perry Mason
Elijah Baley

Harry Dresden
Kinsey Millhone
Bobby Goren
Dr. R. Quincy M.E.
Lenny Briscoe
Shawn Spencer
Inspector Gadget
Jimmy Perez
Lovejoy
Nero Wolfe
Boston Blackie
Cadfael
Lord Peter Wimsey
Inspector Morse
Mac Taylor
Spenser
Mike Hammer
Kojack

Skill, It's What Makes Him Good at This

While you may get away with a Forrest Gump type detective, most readers are looking for someone who will lead the way. Sherlock Holmes, whose vast knowledge of practically everything and superhuman skills at deduction, has captured the imaginations of readers worldwide. Hercule Poirot, Harry Bosch, Veronica Mars, Nancy Drew, Kinsey Millhone, and Charlie Chan are just a few detectives who have awed us with their powers to solve crimes.

Sleuth Skills
Above average intelligence
Reasoning
Super memory
Reading body language

Making sense out of the obscure
Critical thinking and problem solving
Communication skills
Computer/Technology Savvy
Gut Instinct
Perseverance/Determination
Special expertise: firearms expert, forensic entomologist, etc.
Strong sense of right and wrong
Compulsive
Higher standards
Accomplished fighter/martial arts/swordsmanship/etc.
Taking risks
Loyalty
Eye for detail
Experience solving crimes
Side interest: poetry, chess, music, art, wine, etc.
Honesty/Ethics
Knowledge of the Law
Research skills
Controls emotions

You don't want to give your sleuth too many of these attributes. A super sleuth, over the top, can be dull. Pick a few. Find something that is not on the list. Lists are here to help and to inspire. You may find giving an opposite attribute or skill may work better. Perhaps your sleuth does not control her emotions well and is hot-headed. Maybe she works on the dark side of the law, rather than being honest and ethical.

Heroes on the fringe are now popular in this age of the anti-hero. The good guy is not always good. He deals with the bad guys, too. But in the end, the marginal sleuth is there for the cause, righting wrongs, making the world a better place, and finding the bad guy.

Flaws, Nobody Is Perfect

The days of the hero, walking ten feet tall, rescuing kittens, and saving damsels in distress, have passed on. We no longer want our champions walking on water and being perfect. Sleuths from the past had their share of problems and faults. Sherlock Holmes, when faced with insufficient stimulation of his brain, turned to cocaine, a 5% solution, injected intravenously. Hercule Poirot was vain and narcissistic, and rumor has it even his creator, Agatha Christie, had trouble liking him. Inspector Morris drank too much, and Adrian Monk suffered from obsessive-compulsive disorder.

One reason for our love of not so perfect detectives is that we, as readers, realize our shortcomings and can identify with someone who is not on a pedestal. So, don't be afraid to give him or her a flaw.

Some things to consider when choosing your sleuth's flaw.

1. It shall not harm good people.

2. Some hope for redemption or improvement exists.

3. The flaw leads to good things like solving the crime or helping others.

4. The detective's strengths outway his flaws.

5. Deep down the sleuth is a good guy.

6. Some reasonable explanation exists for why she is the way she is.

Point to ponder: the issue with a flawed sleuth is not necessarily an imperfection in itself. Life sucks. Times are hard. Everyone endures hardships and problems. Sometimes it is a fault of the sleuth, and other times he is a victim. The object is creating three-dimensional characters as found in real life.

The Character Flaw List contains items as found in the negative personality list but are more severe. The sleuth would not harm good people, but it certainly drives a wedge between him and others. The character flaw hurts relations and cripples bonds. The failing causes concerns from friends who want to help.

9

Character Flaw List
Abuse
Acts first, thinks later
Alcoholic
Arrogant
Bad habit
Bigot
Cold/aloof
Control freak
Cursed or unlucky
Dishonest
Disorganized
Divorced
Drug addiction
Dyslexic
Eccentricity
Gambling addiction
Grouch
Narcissistic, vain
Obsession
Obsessive-compulsive
Overindulgent
Paranoid
Phobic
Physical challenge, deformity, handicap
Psychological/mental problem, handicap
Rudeness
Self-centered
Stubborn
Superstitious
Temper/anger
Unapologetic
Workaholic

Tidbit: To show the silver lining in a flawed detective, or any character for that matter, have him or her perform an act of kindness. The self-centered, egotistic sleuth gives a child a dollar to buy a candy bar. The grouchy police detective helps save a kitten stranded in a tree. Little things reveal our character's true nature.

Compelling, Rock Stars of Sleuths

A compelling sleuth is one who's an attention grabber. Charismatic. A rock star. The best of his kind. Like him or not, you can't deny, the guy is a good detective.

What makes him the great detective?

- **Larger than life.** Think of James Bond, Sherlock Holmes, and Jay Gatsby. These characters leaped off the pages in literature. What they did was big and grandiose. Readers admired them and wished to be like them.

- **Passion.** The sleuth needs a love for something, for his work. Sherlock Holmes lived and breathed being a detective. Does it have to be just detective work? Nero Wolfe grew orchids and was reported to have 10,000 plants in his greenhouse. Alex Cross played the piano. Harry Bosch loved jazz. But first and foremost, the sleuth is passionate about solving the crime.

- **A yearning or desire, bordering on compulsion.** Again Sherlock Holmes returns to a past love, Irene Adler. Harry Bosch focuses on finding who killed his mother. Cavendish Brown ruminates on his dead wife. Many times this revolves around a death with the detective seeking healing, forgiveness, or retribution. Other things can fill the yearning or desire. Loss of a child or sibling. Remember Fox Mulder in the *X-Files* seeking his sister who'd been taken by aliens? What else falls into this niche? Lost love. Forsaken career. Abandoned goals. But most compelling is the death of someone close.

- **Secrets.** We all love secrets. Something dark. Something hidden. It drives our sleuth to protect himself, puts up barriers, and creates questions needing answers. Walt Longmire, in the series *Longmire,* now on Netflix, kept a dark secret about his wife. Secrets add mystery.

Likable, One Heck of a Guy or Gal

What makes someone likable? You meet her, it clicks, and you like the gal. First and foremost, you see something of yourself in her. She likes jazz music, and you're a fan too. She takes care of an elderly parent, and you have an aging mom. She loves cats, and so do you. Likes attract.

Now the bad news. You cannot write about a sleuth who reflects each of your reader's taste and interests. Besides not knowing them all, giving the sleuth such a vast repertoire of interests and traits would be impossible. But you can go with the next best thing.

Give your sleuth traits associated with good people, people we admire and wish to be like.

Some traits of a likable character (aka your sleuth)
Dependable
Modest
Plays fair
Helpful
Sense of humor
Courageous
Have same goals as us
Truthful
Common sense, street smart
Level headed
Generous
Uncomplaining
Cool-headed
Good listener
Takes responsibility

Respectful
Confident
Compliments others
Consistent
Vulnerable
Optimistic
Genuine
Non-judgmental
Positive attitude
Has values
Friendly, outgoing
Patient
Smiles
Loyal

So if you apply all of these traits to your sleuth, you will have Mother Teresa solving the crime in your novel. Instead, pick a few qualities that make them likable. Don't forget flawed characters. Toss in compelling and a cut above the rest.

Appearance, Hey! I Remember You

Clothes make the man. Kind eyes. Tall, dark and handsome. A real knockout. A sneering smile. Dressed to kill. Almond eyes. Raven black hair. Pouting lips. Buxom blond. Sharp dresser. Dressed to kill. Cute face. Sweet smile. Six-pack abs. Steely eyes. The clichés go on.

Letting your reader know what your sleuth or any character looks like can be significant. People like to know who they are dealing with, but more goes into appearance than just a handful of descriptive words. It may be ironic that many times when a well-known book is made into a movie, the actor playing the sleuth looks nothing like the book version. Guess what? People don't care because looks are only skin deep. (Oops! Another cliché.)

Before getting off the subject, think about Sherlock Holmes in the movies. Many actors have played him. Peter Cushing. Christopher Lee. Basil Rathbone. Johnny Lee. Robert Downy Jr. Benedict Cumberbatch. These guys look nothing alike. Well maybe Cushing, Lee (Christopher) and Rathbone look somewhat like the Sir Arthur Conan Doyle vision, but the bottom line is appearances can be superficial unless they add to the sleuth's character. More on that later.

Aspects of Appearance

Eyes—brown, green, blue, hazel, amber, red, almond, deep-set, hooded, protruding, upturned, downturned, wide-set, close-set, round, mono-lid.

Hair—afro, bob, bouffant, braids, tangled, buzz-cut, brushed, combed, comb-over, corn-rolls, ducktail, pigtails, black, brown, red, blond, white, gray, Auburn, silver, peroxide blond, mousy, ash, brunette, chestnut, carrot top, dirty blond, golden, flaxen, honey, wavy, straight, curly, soft, coarse, wiry, downy, lush, bouncy, springy, straggly.

Lips—thin, thick, full, sexy, pouting, puckered, round.

Chins—round, square, jutting, receding, long, pointy, double, cleft.

Ears—round, square, pointed, narrow, sticking out, attached lobe, broad lobe, no lobe.

Noses—Greek, Roman, hooked, snub, small, turned-up, broad, medium, large.

Skin—dark, light, soft, coarse, smooth, fair, olive, pallor, pasty, peaches-n-cream, rosy, ruddy, white, yellow, tanned, albino, bronzed, black, brown.

Hands—long fingers, stubby fingers, course, calloused, strong, delicate, manly, feminine.

Eyebrows—full, bushy, scant, penciled, uni-brow.

Neck—Swanlike, graceful, lacking, broad, thick.

Body shape and size—tall, short, stout, fat, skinny, thin, husky, muscular, plump, lean.

Clothing—Suits, shirts, ties, ascots, scarves, shoes, Hawaiian shirts, tank top, sleeveless t-shirt, logo t-shirt, blouse, shabby, tattered, toga.

A few words about describing your sleuth. You'll be writing from her point of view. Put yourself in her shoes. She's not thinking: "I have blond hair, blue eyes and a figure to die for." People don't do that in real life, so she won't either. She may look at herself in a mirror and think about her looks. Something might force her to reflect on her appearance. Beyond that, you will have to be smart about how to work in her appearance.

Another thing to consider: find descriptive words that not only define the sleuth's outward appearance but reflect his or her personality. A meticulously dressed man may hint at an obsessive nature. Buzz cut hair and eagle tattoo on the arm may mean ex-military. A woman in stiletto shoes and a tight dress will be different from one in a tank top and straggly hairdo. Make appearances match the character.

Also, description incorporated in action or given with action words will be better received than merely offering of words in a list-like manner.

Character Description Example

Boring

Margaret was tall. She had blue eyes and red hair.

Better

Margaret wore flats rather than high heels to keep from towering over her dates. She once considered wearing green contacts but decided not to when a boyfriend suggested that her blue eyes and red hair reminded him of Molly Ringwald.

Sleuth Example

The next two paragraphs incorporate action as well as meld appearance and personality.

Ace Dawson paused in front of the bathroom mirror and took in his reflection. Three days stubble sprouted on his chin and cheeks. Hair slopped over his ears. He ran his tongue across his teeth. Okay, he'd brush today, and save the haircut and shave for another time.

He snatched the balled-up Hawaiian shirt from the floor and sniffed the armpits. Good enough. He could live with yesterday's breakfast stains on the collar and the unknown smudge on the sleeve. He slipped on the shirt and popped the Panama straw hat on his head. Grabbing his firearm from his nightstand and a donut from an open box on the kitchen table, he headed out for the day.

Do you have a good visual of this guy? Does his appearance define his personality, too?

Likes and Dislikes, It's All Relative

The likes and dislikes of your sleuth and other characters are the subtle things that amplify their persona or may exist for the heck of it. A nervous type detective may drink too much coffee. Your sleuth deep in thought may puff on his pipe. An intellectual may whip out a favorite book of poems during idle hours. One private eye may sleep in late every day, and his partner rises every morning before the sun does.

Yes, likes and dislikes can be to the point of obsessive. Nero Wolfe was quite fond of wine. Sherlock Holmes played the violin and smoked a pipe. Harry Bosch appreciated jazz music. Colombo had a cigar stump tucked between his fingers. Kojack carried a Tootsie Pop with him. As humans, we develop tastes and desires and sometimes aversions.

A like or dislike is a matter of preference and upbringing. One man's poison is another's pleasure. The list that follows is by no means complete but should spur the imagination and offer inspiration. Please feel free to go beyond these items, and by all means expand on it. Your sleuth may not just like cheese but stops every Tuesday at Ma's Deli for a pound of Swiss. Maybe he keeps a cooler of ginger ale soda in his car trunk. Or perhaps she enjoys walking her dog, Moxi, by moonlight on the beach.

Be creative!

Likes and Dislikes
Barbecues
Baseball
Basketball
Beer
Bicycling
Birthdays
Boats
Books
Cabbage
Cake
Camping
Candles
Cats
Cheese
Chinese food
Chocolate
Christmas

Church
Cigarettes
Cigars
Classical music
Climbing
Coffee
Cookies
Cooking
Dogs
Drawing
Fishing
Flowers
Football
Fruits
Gambling
Gardening
Gin
Hugging
Hugs
Humor
Hunting
Ice cream
Jazz music
Junk food
Kisses
Knitting
Making friends
Mondays
Moonlight
Mountains
Movies
Oceans
Painting
Peanut butter and jelly
Picnics
Piercings

Pipes
Pizza
Playing Cards
Popcorn
Pubs/Bars
Rain
Rap
Reggae
Road trips
Rock music
Running
Sewing
Sex
Sleeping in late
Smiling
Snow
Soccer
Soda pop
Sports cars
Sunshine
Surprises
Swimming
Tattoos
Tea
Television
The news
Trains
Traveling
Trees
Video games
Vodka
Walks
Warm weather
Whiskey
Wine

Personality, We All Got To Have It

Personality traits make people who they are. These blend into the other features discussed earlier but can tell so much more about characters. The sleuth is the sum of what has been described so far. But to make him complete toss in a few personality characteristics for good measure.

When choosing traits, select carefully from the positive and negative lists. Consider whether the attributes are compatible with each other and with the qualities of your sleuth.

The following traits are handpicked and by no means complete. Be imaginative and go beyond what is presented here.

Positive Personality Traits
Adventurous
Agreeable
Amiable
Appreciative
Balanced
Brilliant
Calm
Caring
Charming
Cheerful
Clever
Compassionate
Confident
Contemplative
Courageous
Creative
Cultured
Curious
Daring

Dedicated
Dignified
Disciplined
Dramatic
Dynamic
Educated
Energetic
Enthusiastic
Focused
Fun loving
Gallant
Generous
Humble
Humorous
Imaginative
Intelligent
Loyal
Methodical
Moody
Objective
Optimistic
Passionate
Patient
Patriotic
Polished
Protective
Punctual
Relaxed
Responsible
Sexy
Sociable
Optimistic
Strong
Suave
Sweet
Sympathetic

Tidy
Tolerant
Venturesome
Warm
Winning
Wise

Negative Personality Traits
Absentminded
Aggressive
Aloof
Apathetic
Arrogant
Awkward
Biased
Boastful
Boring
Bossy
Callous
Careless
Cheerful
Cold
Compulsive
Cowardly
Cranky
Crude
Cynical
Deceitful
Disorderly
Emotional
Excitable
Fearful
Finicky
Grumpy
Gullible

Ill-tempered
Indifferent
Informal
Insecure
Irresponsible
Jealous
Machiavellian
Moody
Narrow-minded
Nervous
Pessimistic
Prejudiced
Quarrelsome
Resentful
Rigid
Rude
Self-centered
Selfish
Shallow
Sloppy
Sneaky
Stingy
Suspicious
Timid
Torpid
Touchy
Unfriendly
Unimaginative
Uninhibited
Unsuccessful
Vain
Vulgar
Weakling

If you compare the negative traits list to the positive traits list, some trends are noticeable. Characteristics come in pairs. For example, the counterpart of "adventurous" is "timid." But these are not exact opposites. Perhaps, the word was not "timid" you were seeking but "cautious." And again that may not be a negative trait at all. Everything is relative.

As before, let the lists inspire you and help with writer's stall-out. Lists are a beginning to the character development process and not an end.

History, Everyone Has a Past

Your sleuth's history covers everything that happened to him before the story began. This is the place to present life's details. It's a catchall for the personal side of his existence—the sad and the happy moments. The dark secrets. The mundane facts. The good and the bad and the ugly. History is what molded him or her.

Some writers advocate filling in as much detail of the character's life, in this case, your sleuth. History would include information about parents' and siblings' names, high school, hometown, birth date, first love, and so on. I knew one author who kept five-page fill-in-the-blank forms on all her characters.

That may be a bit much. Consider documenting enough information to create a character profile, so he or she feels real. Cover what is essential for the murder mystery you're writing.

I leave the details to you. Here are some areas and features you might want to consider.

Some History Points
A disliked family member
Best friend
Birthplace
Birthdate

Brushes with the law
Childhood nemesis
Children
Close family member
Colleges
Co-workers
Death of loved one
Degrees
Early life
Early friends
Favorite school subjects
Favorite teacher
First friend
First love
Girlfriend/boyfriend
Jobs/Careers
Marriage
Military Service
Neighbors
Parent's names
Prison/Jail time
Schools
Siblings' names
Sexual preference
Tragedies in his or her life
Who inspired him or her
Spouse
Worse thing he or she did
Young adult friends

Details are collected in many ways, and how you do it is your call. Here are a few thoughts.

- Copy the list here. Add anything you might want. Fill it out like a form.

- Pick a few essential items about your sleuth and the novel. Expand them into paragraphs adding needed details.

- Write a short story about your sleuth's history, a few pages tops. Make it his a biography. It does not have to be a top-notch work but contains required material for the murder mystery.

- Write it up for an interview. So tell me Mr. Holmes about your brother Mycroft. Mr. Poirot, tell us about your mother. So, Adrian Monk, how did your wife die?

History Example

In my novel, *The Witch's Daughter*, Book 1 of "A Cavendish Brown Paranormal Mystery" series, I included two critical details of history to help understand the main character and his psyche.

- Cavendish's wife, Emma, had died from cancer the year before the novel's beginning. She had given meaning to his life, and now things were in a downward spiral for him.

- Shortly after graduating high school, Cavendish had broken up with his high school sweetheart, Nikki, over her interest in another boy, and he had run away and joined the army.

Of course, he'd have never met his soul mate, Emma, had he not gone off. Her death had left him emotionally fragile when the story begins. I expanded the details as the novel unfolded and added information to complete the picture over the course of 72,000 words.

Speech, It's How You Say It

The way people speak may be distinctive. Our mannerisms, expressions, and verbal patterns define our characters. Hearing someone talk can immediately identify them. From a conversation, we learn about the speaker. Here are some considerations.

Intelligence

An intelligent person will talk in longer sentences, use bigger and fancier words, and supply more information. An obtuse character will speak more plainly and say dumb things.

Outgoing, Withdrawn

Outgoing characters will be willing to talk and maybe too much. Withdrawn ones may say few words and be reluctant to speak. Motivation to speak relies on many factors. A naturally shy person may not talk much. But someone hiding a secret may also say little.

Speaker's background

People talk about what they know, love, or think about often. Their experience can heavily skew their speech and content. A salesperson may be a smooth talker. A politician will speak eloquently. Our third-grade teacher may talk to people as if they're nine years old. A priest or minister may quote the Bible. A lawyer may put things in legal terms. A gardener may bring up something about his rose bushes or problems with aphids. Knowing your character's experiences and background can skew much about how they talk.

Gestures

Being physical is a trait that defines many people. A woman when she talks touches the shoulder of the listener. A politician provides long handshakes and broad smiles. Some cultures are prone to use more hand gestures while speaking. Body language plays into the mix. Someone being honest may hold their hands out, palms up. Arms folded across the chest can mean withdrawn or hiding something. People have been known to touch their nose or look away when telling a lie.

Regional Language

It distinguishes background and origins. Someone from the Midwest may ask for a glass of pop while in the South it would be a soda. A Southerner asking for sugar may be requesting a kiss, but in the North, they want a sweetener for their iced tea. In some locales, greens refer to salad, in others its collards. "Bless your heart" can mean a sincere appreciation for someone or a way of saying you're an idiot.

Catch Phrases

People have words that pepper their speech. Sometimes they go unnoticed and other times become trademarks. These may be regional or specific to the characters. Having one or two can quickly identify the person and their background. Here are a few examples:

"Aaaay!" (The Fonz from *Happy Days*)

"Bazinga!" (Sheldon from *The Big Bang Theory*)

"I pity the fool." (Mr. T)

"You're fired!" (Donald Trump from *The Apprentice*)

"Hasta la vista, baby!" (Arnold Schwarzenegger from *The Terminator*)

Sleuth Profile

The subgenre/sleuth type defines the sleuth's role. Four qualities go into identifying him or her as a detective with six more covering him or her and other characters (discussed in later chapters). The four sleuth qualities include skills, flaws, compelling, and likable. The six other characteristics deal with name, appearance, likes-dislikes, personality, history, and speech.

When creating your sleuth, finding a name is paramount at the beginning. After all, you can't call him what's-his-name for too long.

Next comes the subgenre/sleuth type. It is the moment you define the kind of mystery you will be writing and the type of sleuth. A cozy, romantic sleuth will be different from a hardboiled P.I. A homicide detective and a sleuthing-medical doctor will define two very different stories.

Then comes skills, flaws, compelling, and likable. You can develop these as you write but they should be laid down early in the story. The sooner you define them, the more likely your audience will begin to identify with your sleuth.

Finally, you want to include appearance, likes-dislikes, personality, history, and speech as the story develops but should start appearing in early chapters. Keep track of them and the other characteristics. There is nothing worse than having a blue-eyed, blond-haired sleuth in chapter one who becomes brown-eyed, brown-haired in chapter nine.

The whole point of this chapter is to come up with a method to create your sleuth simply and yet make a complex character. In some cases, only a few words are required. Others may require some added work with a paragraph or two. Keep in mind that as your write the mystery, your sleuth is going to grow. Areas will expand and develop. Add to your sleuth summary when required.

To recap, here is the outline for your sleuth.

Sleuth Profile
  1. Name
  2. Role, subgenre/sleuth type
  3. Skills
  4. Flaws
  5. Compelling
  6. Likable
  7. Appearance
  8. Likes-dislikes

9. Personality
10. History
11. Speech

Sleuth Profile Example
1. Name—Ace Dawson
2. Role—Hardboiled Detective
3. Skills—super memory, taking risks
4. Flaws—no left hand
5. Compelling—carries a picture of a pretty girl, about 17 years old, in his wallet
6. Likable—plays fair, uncomplaining
7. Appearance—unshaven most of the time, needs a haircut, wears Hawaiian shirts and a Panama hat
8. Likes and Dislikes—drinks only ginger ale, no alcohol, often eats at Ma's Deli
9. Personality—nervous, moody
10. History—lost hand during bombing while serving in Iraq, best friend is Mackey Wilcox, the bookie
11. Speech—catchphrase = "I should have listened to Mother and become a doctor."

This is a start for Ace, but things can change. I'll update his profile in my notes and track the changes. Maybe it's his left foot that's missing; he wears a porkpie hat and Mother wanted him to be an accountant. Time will tell.

Chapter Three:
The Victim

The Crime

Most mysteries are murder stories. Somebody is found dead. A crime has been committed. The sleuth finds the killer. But other types of mysteries can be written.

Mystery Types
Murder
Kidnapping
Missing persons
Theft
Blackmail
Caper
Extortion
Child molestation/pornography

In all cases, there is a victim. Someone disappeared or was kidnapped. Something of great value was taken from someone. Blackmail money collected. Many times, the "lesser" crime leads to murder.

This book will mostly talk about the "murder mystery." But it's not far removed from other crimes with similar features. A sleuth. A victim. Suspects. A final reckoning for the crime.

Murder is the most heinous crime in our society and perhaps the most fascinating. Homicides hit the top of daily feeds and make headlines. We may skip over much of the news, brushing past sports, finance, politics (well maybe not these days!), tech and health, but come murder our full attention is focused.

In the murder mystery, someone dies early in the novel. The murder can happen on the first page, in the first few chapters, and perhaps even before the beginning of the book. Cold case murders where the victim died years and even decades earlier are popular. There is no hard rule when the crime happens. Some advice says to have the death in the first ten pages. Early in the book is a good idea. What is essential: give the reader a story and provide them with the murder as soon as possible.

In the cozy mystery, the murder typically happens off stage. Violence is played down. The reader comes more for the excitement of a whodunit and not for sensationalism.

In the police procedural, the murder is upfront and out there. It is a no holds barred approach. Many times it's related to a street murder, a robbery gone wrong, a crime of passion.

For the private investigator, the murder falls out of an investigation. The P.I. may be following a wayward husband only to find the guy killed by underworld types. Or digging into corporate espionage leads to the death of an innocent accountant.

Tidbit: 80% of murders are committed by a friend, relative, or acquaintance.

Backstory for Victim

The victim has a backstory that ties him or her to the killer and the crime. The depth of it may be small or complex. The backstory can use the sleuth's and other character's emotions.

During a bank robbery, someone kills the guard. Not much backstory may be needed. The bank guard has no real connection to the robbers or killer, but he has a history. Perhaps he was married, had a small child, and was going to night school to become a respiratory therapist. Now it plays off the sleuth's sympathy and the readers too.

The owner of a local trucking company is found dead, shot while sitting in his office. He had a business partner, a trophy wife, an unhappy teenage son, an irate customer, a girlfriend with drug addiction, an aging mother in a nursing home, a cash-strapped sister, an alcoholic brother-in-law. This guy's life was a mess, and his backstory sounds like an epic tale.

You need to give the victim as much backstory as is required to tell the tale and link him to the crime. It is something not to be dumped all at once but put out in bits and pieces as discovered by the sleuth.

Victim Backstory Ideas are meant here to stir the imagination. The subject may apply directly to the victim or someone he knows.

Victim Backstory Ideas
Alcoholism
Bad choices
Blackmail
Business
Career
Cheating
Children
Crime
Death
Drugs
Loneliness
Love triangle
Lover dispute
Mental illness
Money
Past identity
Politics
Power
Religion
Romance
Sickness
Success/Failure
Unhealthy relationships

Try picking something from the list and adding a bit of imagination. Perhaps combine two or more things. Be inventive and find some new angle.

Crime and Death Example

Roberto drove a getaway car for a bank robbery. Two people died during the heist. He served twenty years in prison. Now he tries to put the past behind him.

Romance and Religion Example

Carl fell in love with a beautiful woman. She belonged to a religious cult. He tried to fit in with them, but things got too strange. He had to make a choice and left her behind. Later she died during some religious rite.

Career and Alcoholism Example

Magda was a thriving middle manager at a manufacturing firm. She had an affair with the boss, a married man. They broke it off. She was devastated and began drinking. Later, she lost her job.

Most past events that affect the present and lead to murder are negative influences. No one kills a successful person with a great spouse, beautiful children, and loyal friends. The exception would be a random killing, perhaps during a robbery or some other event where someone is in the wrong place at the wrong time.

Victim's Secrets

Backstory leads to secrets. Secrets happen between the victim and the suspects (remembering the killer is a suspect until the end). These secrets lead to murder. The sleuth's job is to discover the secrets using clues and find the killer. The keyword here is secrets, things kept between typically two people, not to be shared.

How does it work? The backstory leads to someone else becoming involved. It may not be just the victim's backstory but that of the killer that leads to murder. Later we will discuss the killer in detail and motive for murder. But everything comes back to secrets.

If in real estate the key is location, location, location, then in the murder mystery it's secrets, secrets, secrets.

Returning to the earlier examples, let's add the secret.

Crime and Death Example

Roberto drove a getaway car or a bank robbery. Two people died during the heist. He served twenty years in prison. Now he tries to put the past behind him. Roberto rebuilds his life with a lovely wife, two small children, and a thriving small motor repair business. Bart, a fellow convict, shows up after getting out of prison and threatens to expose Roberto's past, ruining his business prospects and possibly rocking his marriage. The two fight, and the ex-con bludgeons Roberto with a wrench from the business's workshop.

Romance and Religion Example

Carl fell in love with a beautiful woman. She belonged to a cult. He tried to fit in with them, but things got too strange. He had to make a choice and left her behind. Later she died during a religious rite. Years later after Carl has rebuilt his life, Maggie, the sister of the dead girl, shows up. They seem to hit it off and begin to date. Of course, she does not tell him about her sister but blames him for her sister's death. Carl dies, poisoned, while the two have a romantic dinner.

Career and Alcoholism Example

Magda was a thriving middle manager at a manufacturing firm. She had an affair with the boss, a married man. They broke it off. She was devastated and began drinking. She lost her job. Her old boss comes back in her life now, working at another company. They resume their affair. When she learns that he is using her with no chance to make good on his promises, she threatens to go to his wife. He kills her with a knife from her kitchen.

No Mr. Nice Guy

Often the victim is disliked. As the sleuth digs into the suspects' background, he learns nobody liked the victim. Most of the negativity is justifiable. Not-so-nice people become targets for potential murderers.

Reason for not being nice
Doesn't play well with others
Self-centered
A Bully
Mean-streak
Power hungry
Takes advantage for personal gain
Insulting
Disagreeable
Being a jerk
Narcissistic
Rude
Defensive
Narrow-minded
Insecure

Superior
Opinionated
Selfish
Oversized ego

Looking through this list, a common theme emerges. *Me first, you don't count.*

These attributes overlap those in the negative trait list from the section on personality and may be used when defining the victim's character. But the key to using them is to roll them into the backstory and secrets.

"No Mr. Nice Guy" Example

Mr. McCann, a wealthy man, was found dead, shot once through the heart. Recently, he had changed his will, cutting out his nephews Huey and Bart, leaving his fortune to his mistress, Amy Ashe, and his cat, Mr. Tibbs. Also, Mr. McCann fired his butler, Wadsworth, when he accused the servant of stealing. So, three unhappy people are suspects because the victim was not nice to them. And one person, Amy, is also a suspect, perhaps killing him for the money. Maybe he was not nice to her after all; sleuthing may reveal a rocky relationship between her and McCann. For now we will assume the kitty is not a suspect.

More on Names

Much planning went into finding the sleuth's name. For other characters, a more generic approach may be taken. Important is discovering a name that fits the character and is easily remembered by the reader.

Name Sources

Back in the day, phone books made good references for names. Now, Internet searches work well. Go to your favorite search engine. Check out "Surnames starting with X" or "First names that begin with X" where X=an alphabet letter.

If this doesn't find you a name, think of people you know—friends, relatives, co-workers, neighbors, TV/Movie personalities, the news . . . you get the picture. Don't copy directly. Mix things up a bit. The mechanic who worked on your car is Bill Maize. The lady who checks you out at Walmart has Mindy Johnson on her name tag. Your character's name becomes Mindy Maize.

Imagination always works well, too. Be inventive.

Location

Is the character from France or have a French Heritage? Maybe he lives in Alabama. Modify the Internet search. "French first names beginning with X." "Southern first names beginning with X."

Fit name to the character

A rich man will have a different sounding name than a good ole boy from North Carolina. Richard Todd Bennett and Bubba Jones. You can quickly tie the name with the man. Research it. Hear it. Write it. How does it fit the character? His profession? His social status?

Age and Era

Names change with time. What was popular in one era may be outdated in another. More Internet searches. "Popular boy names in the 1980's." Answers are Michael, Christopher, and Matthew. "Popular girl names in the 17th century." Results are Anne, Catherine, and Charlotte.

Neutral names

Don't get fancy. Frank Barnes and Millie Cramer work well. But if you need Alexander Mikhailov or Jakub Przybyszewski, go for it.

The name's sound

Can you and your reader live with it for 200-plus pages?

Helpful hints when naming and using names

- Introduce characters slowly. A character or two per chapter works well. Too many too soon will confuse the reader.

- Avoid similar sounding names for characters. Mickey and Mikey will give the reader fits. Jimmy and Timmy will add confusion.

- Alphabet assignment. Write the alphabet down the side of the page. Assign the names, only one per letter. This will help the reader and avoid conflicts.

- Stick to one name. Let's say you name your character Robert J. Jones, FBI agent. Writers have tendencies to find different words for the same thing. So when referring to him, he can be Robert, Bobby, Bob, Rob, Jones, R.J., the agent, the FBI agent. All those names will confuse the reader. What you call him should be the same on every page and chapter.

- Go with the POV character. Your scenes will be from his or her viewpoint. Think how he or she will see the other characters. In my Penelope Mystery Series, her uncle is always Uncle Elmer and her parents, Mother and Father. People see their friends and family by first names. Professionals in many fields use last names. Childhood friends and close friends may be known by their nickname or diminutive name. Robert becomes Bobby. Jennifer is Jen or Jenny. Sometimes children modify names; Robert White is called Whitey by his friends. Al McIntosh is Mac to his boyhood buddies. Older family members may see younger ones by formal first names like James or Arthur. But whatever you pick, stick with it.

- The exception to the "stick to one name" rule comes when switching point-of-view in a scene. The POV character will see things with the name he or she is familiar with. A child will see Mom while her father will see Ruthie. In my "Cavendish Brown Paranormal Mystery" series, most POV characters see "Alex," but her mother always sees "Alexandra." Be cautious and do not confuse.

Victim Profile

For developing the sleuth, eleven characteristics are defined. Five of those apply to other characters including the victim. These include appearance, likes and dislikes, personality, history, and speech. The same rules of assigning characteristics apply. Just apply them as needed to define the character.

Backstory and secrets need to be included. It is what ties back to the plot and to the suspects, most importantly the killer. Note: while I covered backstory and secrets in two section, they really are linked and should be thought of that way.

Use the following outline for the victim.

Victim Profile
1. Name
2. Role, victim
3. Backstory/secrets
4. Appearance, as needed
5. Likes-dislikes, as needed
6. Personality, as needed
7. History, as needed
8. Speech, as needed

Why Does the Sleuth Want to Solve the Crime?

Most mystery writers starting out do not give this aspect much thought, but the reality is your sleuth must have a reason to get involved. Doing it just for the heck of it won't fly. Solving crimes is not a good hobby. If boredom is the reason, surely better ways exist to shake it up. Plus finding a killer has lots of downsides. It takes your sleuth away from whatever pays the rent. He or she probably has better things to do. Putting one's life on the line is not smart without a good cause.

Maybe it's your sleuth's job. She is a homicide detective and gets the assignment to find the killer. Good start! But ratchet up things. Make it personal. Perhaps the killer starts to send threats to the detective. Phone calls come with deep breathing. Creepy little gifts arrive at her apartment. Another body appears with a "love" note. The captain wants to take her off the case, but she insists she can do it.

For the cozy mystery sleuth, he may be a retired school teacher. His best friend has been charged with the murder. Your sleuth could be playing gin rummy with his buddies at the VFW, but now he has to do something. He and his buddy have known each other since high school, were best man at each other's weddings, and godfather's to each other's first born. Things have become personal. He has to clear his friend of the charges.

The Private Eye may have started out investigating some missing jewelry thought to have been taken by his client's maid. Instead, he uncovers a plot to steal her fortune. Then someone murders her, and the bullet comes from his revolver. He must clear his name while on the lam from the police.

Bottom line: give your sleuth an excellent reason to solve the crime.

Reasons to solve a murder
- The sleuth witnessed the killing, but no one believes him or her.
- A professional detective whose job is to solve the crime.
- The sleuth may be the next victim
- A friend, relative, or lover of the sleuth may be the next victim.
- The victim was a friend, relative, or lover.
- The next victim may be a friend, relative, or lover.
- Someone asked the sleuth for help.
- The sleuth is a private detective and does it for money.
- The crime has personal meaning to the sleuth.
- A threat against the sleuth, a friend, a relative, or a lover.
- The sleuth appears to be the killer.

Is it history or backstory?

The answer is simple. Backstory is needed to drive the plot. The story only makes sense when the victim's, suspects', and killer's backstories are included. History is the baggage a character brings along that may amplify and explain him or her but is not necessary to the plot.

For example, the sleuth tries to help a middle-aged woman after she was mugged. She struggles to raise her nephew which reminds him of his aunt who raised him until he was nineteen when she died in a botched robbery. While it helps explain his reactions and feelings, it is not necessary to solve the crime. His history can be left out, and the story would still move forward.

The beautiful thing about the sleuth's history is it makes for a well-rounded, three-dimensional character. Readers feel closer to him or her. His life is their life. His world, theirs.

In contrast, the victim's backstory is required to better understand the crime. An accountant is found shot, his body stuffed in an oil drum. Backstory tells us he worked for a drug cartel, laundering money. That is a significant clue to his murder. But perhaps it is just a red herring. This is the fun part of writing and reading mysteries.

Should your victim or other characters have a history? Yes, to round out their role. Should they have backstory? When it's needed to drive the plot.

To summarize: backstory is history, but not all history is backstory.

A Last Thought on the Victim

In Volume One of the series "Writing the Killer Mystery," five elements were introduced to model the mystery story. Central is the "The Crime." But in concluding this chapter, the crime and the victim are synonymous. Defining one includes the other.

Other elements in the story model are the sleuth, the perpetrator, other characters, and the setting. Moving forward, much of the focus will be the murder mystery, and the perpetrator will be the killer.

The following diagram becomes the Murder Mystery Story Model with these slight modifications. Although the mystery is typically considered to be a plot-driven story, the characters along with the setting anchor the story and add depth.

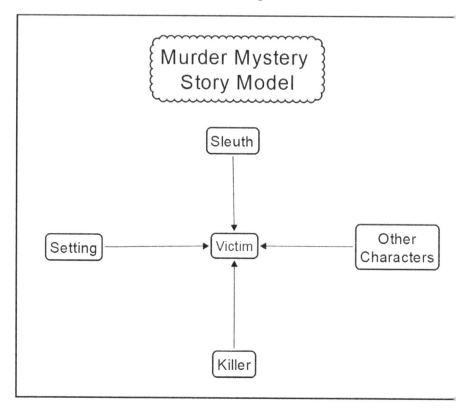

Mystery Story Model
1. The Victim
2. The Sleuth
3. The Killer
4. The Other Characters
5. The Setting

Chapter Four:
The Killer

Supervillain Skills

If you did your homework, you are on your way to having a super sleuth. That is what makes good mystery stories. People buy them for the detective. And if he or she is topnotch, then the killer better be, too!

What makes a worthy adversary? Think of the movies and books and TV shows, the ones we could not wait to see what happens next. Goldfinger vs. James Bond. Lord Voldemort vs. Harry Potter. Joker vs. Batman. Hannibal Lecter vs. Clarice Starling. Professor Moriarty vs. Sherlock Holmes. Thinking of the famous villain-hero combinations brings a shiver of excitement.

The answer to the question is simple. A villain must be worthy of your super sleuth. Killers have their skills, too.

Supervillain Skills
Ambitious
Arrogant
Beautiful
Boastful
Charming
Cold hearted
Confident
Cool-headed
Crafty
Cruel
Cultured
Cunning
Curious
Demanding

Determined
Egotistical
Extravagant
Eye for detail
Fanatical
Flamboyant
Genius
Goal-focused
Handsome
Honest
Immoral
Intelligent
Judgmental
Management skills
Manipulative
Mental/psychological problems
Motivated
Narrow-minded
Obsessive
Opinionated
Organized
Poor Loser
Possessive
Powerful/strong
Predatory
Psychopath/Sociopath
Ruthless
Secretive
Sense of humor
Smart
Strong sense of justice
Survivor
Uncommon dresser
Unique background
Vengeful
Violent

In most mysteries, the murderer is not revealed until the end of the book, so exercise some care when applying these characteristics and not tip your hand early. You want your killer to blend in with the other suspects for much of the book. Also, the suspects may possess some diluted version of these skills.

In the end, the bad guy will be extreme regarding supervillain skills. Exceptionally resourceful. Warped sense of humor. Relentlessly determined. Knockout beautiful. Keeping it hidden until the story end and conveying the supervillain skill is the trick.

Show the supervillain skill without directly associating it with him or her. The victim may have been left dead in an unusual manner, spelling out a cruel or sadistic killer. Maybe he posed the body propped in a chair, wearing a clown nose and funny hat. The police determine the killer was an ex-KGB assassin. Doing something that says "wow, this is a really a bad guy" can push your book to the top of the charts.

Associate the supervillain skill with the perpetrator near the end of the novel. The sleuth uncovers the murderer's identity but may be too late because he too is now a possible victim. The bad guy has set in motion an ultimate murder plan targeting someone special or a group of people. The perpetrator leads the detective on a wild chase where it looks as if he may escape. Make the killer's reveal exciting and suspenseful with a possibility the sleuth has failed. (Of course, he doesn't.)

The police procedural is the exception to the reveal at the end policy where sometimes the killer is exposed sooner. In this case, more can be done to exploit the supervillain characteristics. This can lead to a spectacular ending.

Sticking to one or two traits is wise. Too many and the character will start sounding like a comic book supervillain. Sometimes only one trait is needed. Being a psychopath is sufficient to propel your bad guy to the top of the ten most wanted.

Murderer's Backstory and Secrets

The murderer and the victim will share a backstory. It's what they have in common. Recall the three examples from earlier.

- Bart and Roberto both were ex-cons who had served time together with Bart threatening to expose Roberto's past.

- Maggie blames Carl for her sister's death, the backstory they both shared.

- Magda and her boss have an affair with him using her.

Often in the real world, the murderer and victim do not share a backstory. A robber kills a bank teller. A drug addict shoots a man during a holdup. A serial killer strangles a woman in an alley. Yet, when writing a story, giving them a common backstory can make it so much more exciting and personal. The bank teller was the robbers inside person who he believed double-crossed him. The addict kills a man who happens to be his mother's new boyfriend. The killer picks only women with blond hair and green eyes because they remind him of his mother who deserted him when he was twelve.

Secrets may be shared by the victim and murderer or belong to one of them. The bank teller planned a romantic getaway with one of the robbers after the holdup. The boyfriend is actually the addict's father who had returned to his mother after twenty years. The woman snuffed by the killer was his long-lost sister, hence why she looked like mom.

Killer Profile

The same commonality exists between all characters such as likes-dislikes, personality, history, and speech. Mix in supervillain skills, backstory, and secrets, and you have a recipe for a topnotch killer.

Killer Profile
1. Name
2. Role, killer
3. Backstory/secrets
4. Supervillain skills
5. Appearance, as needed
6. Likes-dislikes, as needed
7. Personality, as needed
8. History, as needed
9. Speech, as needed

Murderer Example
1. Name—William Franklin Asher
2. Role—killer
3. Backstory/secrets—he had an affair with one of his patients. His receptionist, Ann Hathaway found out. Most of his money comes from his wife's family, and fearing she'd expose him, he killed Ann.
4. Super Villain Characteristics—cunning and flamboyant
5. Appearance—tall, six foot three. Silver hair. Wry smile.
6. Likes-dislikes—Cuban cigars. Single malt Scotch.
7. Personality—fun loving guy who likes to spend money and have good times,
8. History— Ph.D., psychologist. Met his wife while an undergraduate. She helped fund his degree.
9. Speech—noticeable Texas drawl.

Crazy Killers

Psychopaths and sociopaths appear in the Supervillain Skills list. It has become quite common to depict cold-blooded murderers as psychopaths. Though not as common in cozy mysteries, a police procedural may follow a serial killer, typically described as a psychopath and sometimes a sociopath.

Psychopath Characteristics
Superficial charm that radiates confidence
Inflated sense-of-self
Pathological liar
Manipulative
No guilt or remorse
No deep emotions
Lacking empathy
Impulsive
Irresponsible
Short-term marital relationships
History of juvenile delinquency/behavioral problems
Breaks rules, believes himself above authority
No personal ethics

In the real world, many psychopaths function quite well. They may only display a few of these characteristics. The psychopath may maintain a marriage but continually lies to his or her spouse. He or she may keep a good job but sees no issue with destroying others on the way up the corporate ladder. In fact, because of their charming personality, high self-confidence, and manipulative behavior, many psychopaths are CEOs of companies.

But they also make great killers. Do not be afraid to have one in your next novel.

A quick word on sociopaths, aka Antisocial Personality Disorder: they share many traits with psychopaths but function less well in society, having fits of rage, being disorganized, living on the fringe of society, and being antisocial. Think of the charming killer who smooth-talks his victims into going away with him, only to brutally murder them; that would be a psychopath. Now take the crude hermit living in the woods who captures hikers and campers to hang them by their heels on meat hooks and slash their throats; that would be a sociopath.

Unless you need to have some Ph.D. type in your story analyze the behavior of the killer, just grab some of the characteristics from the psychopath list and use them in the Killer Profile. The character you create will be memorable.

Chapter Five:
The Suspects

Why Suspects Are Like The Killer

Until the moment of truth, when your sleuth does the big reveal, the killer is another suspect. In the beginning, no difference exists between them, at least from the reader's perspective. As the sleuth collects clues, discoveries are made, and secrets revealed, the focus will turn to the killer, but until then he will blend in with the other suspects.

Therefore, the suspects will have backstory and secrets that intersect the victim as well as each other and the killer. The backstory and secrets may share some commonality with the killer and victim, or they may be unique and different. The job of your sleuth will be to sort out the data and make sense of it.

Like the killer, the suspects will hide information, lie, and do bad things. Initially, they may look as guilty as the killer. This makes work for the detective and fun for the reader. Don't make it too easy for the sleuth.

Why Suspects Are Not Like the Killer

As your sleuth snoops and asks questions and finds clues, he or she will eliminate suspects. Perhaps the suspect has a good alibi. Or maybe he doesn't have a good reason to kill the victim. Clues may point toward someone else. Ultimately the sleuth will eliminate the suspects for one reason or another until only one guilty person remains.

It will be the killer.

Suspect's Profile

The suspect will have characteristics similar to the murderer with one exception. He or she will lack the supervillain skills. Not saying you can't toss it into the mix, but then there was something special about the killer. Best to keep it that way.

The suspect's character will still include name, role, backstory/secrets, appearance, likes and dislikes, history, and speech. Some of these are listed "as needed" but adding them and building on them is still recommended. Enough must be added to avoid flat characters who go through the motions like a bad actor following a script.

Suspect Profile
1. Name
2. Role, suspect
3. Backstory/secrets
4. Appearance, as needed
5. Likes-Dislikes, as needed
6. Personality, as needed
7. History, as needed
8. Speech, as needed

Chapter Six:
Special Characters

The Sidekick

Not necessary, but supplying your sleuth with a sidekick can have benefits. Many famous detectives had sidekicks with some duos being nearly inseparable. Mention Sherlock Holmes and John Watson comes to mind. Sgt. Joe Friday always had Officer Bill Gannon at his side. Adrian Monk kept his assistant near.

Does your sleuth need a buddy? Contemplate this.

- Everybody needs a sounding board. A confidant. Ultimately your detective will want somebody to talk to and try out ideas. The sidekick is this guy.

- Alternate viewpoint. Your sleuth spouts his latest theory of the killer's method, and the sidekick chimes, "Yes, but what if…" The sleuth says black, and the sidekick replies could be white. Up, maybe down. High, perhaps low. Opposite viewpoints keep the possibilities open.

- Ever need your brain picked? A good sidekick will ask questions. Need further explanations. Push for exemplification. It keeps the story going, but the real reason is to keep your readers informed.

- Scenes flow better with two people. Yes, it can be a single character, just the sleuth, but toss in another person, the sidekick, and things go smoothly. They can talk and argue and discuss the clues. He can watch your sleuth's back. Do some grunt work. And be there for support.

- Off camera details. The sidekick loves errands (maybe) and can take care of tasks too mundane for the detective and uninteresting for the reader. Time passes, and the sidekick returns with the information, missing evidence, a sudden revelation to keep the plot moving. Don't even have to cover much great detail how he did it.

What do you need for a great sleuth-sidekick combo? Chemistry. Detective soulmates. Your duo needs to complement each other, the sidekick playing against the sleuth. If he is cold and calculating, the sidekick is warm and candid. A moody, stuffy sleuth needs a steady, laid-back assistant. Genius thinker vs. everyday guy. A rude, arrogant sleuth needs a polite, humble helper. Opposites attract. Balance, balance, balance. This should not be a formula but return to the idea of partners in solving crimes.

Some characteristics of a Sidekick
Loyal/faithful
Supportive
A cheerleader
A friend
An assistant
Good listener
Talented/goal oriented

Famous Detective-Sidekick Duos
Sherlock Holmes—John Watson
Hercule Poirot—Arthur Hastings
Martin Beck—Gunvald Larsson
Master Li—Number Ten Ox
Sister Fidelma—Brother Eadulf
Hildegarde Withers—Inspector Oscar Pipe
Spenser—Hawk
Perry Mason—Della Street, Paul Drake
Sgt. Joe Friday—Officer Bill Gannon
Green Hornet—Kato
Batman—Robin
Lord Peter Wimsey—Mervyn Bunter
Albert Campion—Magersfontein Lugg

Precious Ramotswe—Grace Makutsi
Adrian Monk—Sharona Fleming, later Natalie Teeger
Charlie Chan—Number One Son
Nero Wolfe—Archie Goodwin
Inspector Darko Dawson—Philip Chikata
Inspector Morse—Sergeant Lewis
Inspector Thomas Lynley—Sergeant Barbara Havers
Dave Robicheaux—Clete Purcel
DI Jimmy Perez—DS Alison McIntosh

The Opponent

The opponent is the guy or gal that upsets the sleuth, gets in the way, creates obstacles, makes life difficult, and is annoying. The opponent may be a great person, but the sleuth doesn't like him or her. Maybe the opponent deserves the sleuth's animosity, maybe he doesn't.

Sherlock Holmes' nemesis is Detective Inspector Greg Lestrade of Scotland Yard. Lestrade respects Holmes and seeks his advice, but Holmes looks down on him and insults him.

In the police procedural, this is the fellow detective who always conflicts with the sleuth, trying to one-up him or her in investigations and steal the glory. This rocky relationship is well known throughout the division and may even lead to warnings from superiors.

In the cozy, the sleuth's opponent can be a local police detective. The amateur detective gets warnings to stay clear of the crime scene and stop meddling. Of course, he or she doesn't listen, and friction increases.

For the private eye, an ex-wife can make an annoying opponent. She shows up at inopportune moments, asks for back alimony, and wants him to listen to her sob-story. He tries to blow her off and get back to work, but she persists her needling ways.

The opponent's action aims at the sleuth, not the story. Their relationship is based on friction. If it affects other things like the story progress then so be it.

Some Characteristics of an Opponent
Competition
Jealousy
Mutual dislike
Superior-Inferior
Personality Clash
Class status
Conflict of interests
Bad influence

The Supporter

The supporter is the go-to person when things get tough. When we are young, we go to mom or dad and spell out our woes. In return, we get a sympathetic ear, advice, and encouragement. It is the same for the sleuth.

For the police detective, a superior like the captain or division head is available to discuss a case or listen to some personal problem. The cozy sleuth has an old buddy or spouse ready to listen and offer advice. The private eye seeks solace with his bartender or priest. The key is someone who'll listen.

An excellent example comes from the TV series "Justified" about Deputy US Marshal Raylan Givens, who flirts with both sides of the law and sometimes shoots first and asks questions later. His superior, Chief Deputy Art Mullen, has an open door policy, where the two often meet to discuss Raylan's actions and misdeeds. Sometimes Art reprimands Raylan and reminds him of the correct direction. Of course, much of their discourse happens over a bottle of Kentucky bourbon.

Some Characteristics of a Supporter
Good listener
Offer advice
Friend
Moral compass
Teacher
Positive influence
Role model

Sidekick, Opponent, and Supporter Profiles

The profile of these characters will include the relationship between them and the sleuths. It may cover all or just a few of the characteristics noted above and perhaps something new.

Special Character Profile

1. Name

2. Role as Sidekick, Opponent, Supporter

3. Appearance, as needed

4. Likes-Dislikes, as needed

5. Personality, as needed

6. History, as needed

7. Speech, as needed

Chapter Seven:
The Rest of the Cast

Major and Minor Character

Going beyond the main characters, which includes the sleuth, the murderer, the victim, suspects, and special characters, are the major and minor ones. In movie credits, these players come after the headliners. It is not to diminish their importance, but in many cases, the minor characters may have simple monikers as "Nosey Neighbor," "Policeman 1," "Policeman 2," and so forth.

Although these actors hold perhaps less status than the main characters, they still demand some thought and planning to get them right. Key here is to make all of the parts three-dimensional and pay close attention to the major players.

Major Character

- Appears frequently in scenes
- Has roles that move the plot forward
- Can be part of subplots
- Can be the point-of-view in a scene
- Complex or rounded persona

Minor Character

- Appears less frequent
- May or may not influence plot progress
- No subplots of their own
- No POV
- Simple or flat persona
- May have no contact with the sleuth

Fleshing out either group is done by following the basic profile outline. Major characters receive more attention than minor ones. While most characteristics in the profile are considered for the major character, the minor one may only need one or two. Not even a name is necessary. Just calling him the waiter or her the hostess is enough. A word or two on appearance or personality is sufficient.

Major and Minor Profiles
1. Name, not needed for Minor Characters
2. Role, Major or Minor Character
3. Appearance, as needed
4. Likes-Dislikes, as needed
5. Personality, as needed
6. History, as needed
7. Speech, as needed

Note on backstory/secrets: while major and minor characters may have some connection by association, the details would be tracked within the profiles of the victim, the killer, and the suspects. For example, the purchase of a revolver from a gun shop by the killer would be tracked under the killer's profile and not the gun shop owner's. If for some reason, the connection is more than just association, then the major or minor character may actually be a suspect, assuming the killer and victim are already established in the plot.

Chapter Eight:
Creating the Players in Your Mystery Novel

Creating Characters

Ask a dozen writers how they track characters, and you'll get as many methods. How you manage them is your call but here are few suggestions.

- At a minimum, use the profiles suggested in this volume to document your characters. Only a few words or a sentence or two in each category will do.

- As your story progresses, update the character's profile. You may not know it when starting, but perhaps by mid-book, your sleuth has blue eyes. Document it. Near the end of the story, the sleuth's mother's name is revealed; add that too.

- Devote a sheet or page to each character. Start a file system. Keep a journal. Find some method to manage the characters' attributes.

- One way to understand your character is writing a few pages in the first person from his or her viewpoint. Tell a short story. Describe something in the character's life. Make it his or her manifesto.

- The combination of suspects, special characters, and major/minor characters make up the "other characters" element of the Murder Mystery Story Model.

- Last suggested method is a freeform profile. Start with the character's name and follow with attributes, creating a quick glance chart. This method works well when keeping notes by hand in a journal. At the character develops, more traits are tacked onto the growing list.

Freeform Character Example

Ace Dawson
Hardboiled Detective
Super memory, takes risks
Missing left hand
Carries a picture of a pretty girl about 17 years old in his wallet
Plays fair, uncomplaining
Unshaven, needs a haircut, wears Hawaiian shirts and a Panama hat
Drinks only ginger ale, no alcohol, often eats Ma's Deli
Nervous, moody
Lost hand during bombing while serving in Iraq
Best friend is Mackey Wilcox, a local bookie
Catchphrase— "I should have listened to Mother and become a doctor."
Spends Saturdays at greyhound races, never wins much
Father left the family when Ace was six.
"Ace" is a nickname; his actual first name is Arthur
Scar above right eye

Note this list of characteristics follows the earlier profile for Ace Dawson. But more items have been added as the character developed. The freeform version makes updating a profile easier although finding a particular tidbit might take some reviewing.

Mind Map Example

Some find a mind map useful. Here is Ace Dawson from earlier with the categories of role, skills, flaws, compelling, likable, backstory/secrets, appearance, likes/dislikes, personality, history, and speech. Sub categories have been filled in according to the freeform profile shown earlier.

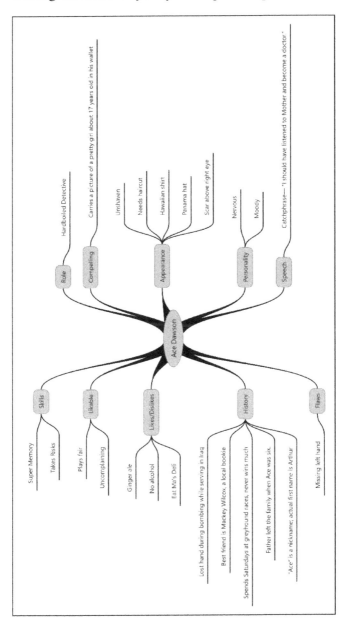

Designing Characters

The following summarizes profiles for characters and can be used to create a fill in the blank form and a guide to creating players for your mystery novel.

Name—required for all characters, use descriptor for minor characters.

Role—defines character role: subgenre/sleuth type, victim, killer, suspect, sidekick, opponent, supporter, major/minor character.

Skills—required only for sleuth or killer.

Flaws—required only for sleuth.

Compelling—required only for sleuth.

Likable—required only for sleuth.

Backstory/Secrets—required only for victim, killer, suspects.

Appearance—for all characters, only as needed**.

Likes/Dislikes—for all characters, only as needed**.

Personality—for all characters, only as needed**.

History—for all characters, only as needed**.

Speech—for all characters, only as needed**.

** Appearance, likes/dislikes, personality, history, speech need only be included to portray a rounded character. A minor character may only need one or two. Major characters three or four. Other characters five or more. Keep in mind the type of the character required for the mystery novel. More details will only add more the character depth.

Mystery Novel Character Design

Name:	
Role:	
Skills:	
Flaws:	
Compelling:	
Likable:	
Backstory/Secrets:	
Appearance:	
Likes/Dislikes:	
Personality:	
History:	
Speech	

Character Lists

This volume focused on choosing traits from lists or as supplied from you the author. Those traits populated categories and formed lists to profile your characters. The categories become less important than the actual attribute and in many cases some overlap may be seen. Ultimately, Character Lists can be used to easily and rapidly describe the personalities of the players in your mystery novel with an unique set of traits.

Chapter Nine: Last thoughts

Just a Few Words, Please

Thank you for taking the time to read *Writing the Killer Mystery: Captivating Characters, Volume Two*. The plan laid out here is a sure way to create characters for your mystery novel. If I've helped and you found this useful, please let others know and leave a few words on Amazon about the book. The link below is provided for your convenience.

https://amzn.to/2s1MvVv

Writing the Killer Mystery Series

Volume 1: Great Beginnings (Released April 2018)

- Mystery Writers and Their Sleuths
- Understanding the Mystery
- Types of Mystery
- Got a good idea?

Volume 2: Captivating Characters (Released May 2018)

- The Sleuth
- The Victim
- The Killer
- The Suspects
- Special Characters

- The Rest of the Characters

Volume 3: Plotting the Murder (July 2018)

- The Plot
- The Opening
- The Middle Game
- The End
- Scenes

Volume 4: Places, Clues, and Guilt (October 2018)

- Setting
- Means, Motive, Opportunity
- Clues, Red Herrings, Misdirection
- History, Backstory

Volume 5: Getting it Right, Getting Paid (January 2019)

- Writing Advice
- Revision
- Publishing
- Promotion

Note: release dates and content of future volumes are subject to change. Please stop my website at http://www.authorrondvoigts.com for updates.

About Ron D. Voigts

Ron writes murder mysteries. His sleuths have included a thirteen-year-old, a psychic, a news reporter, a playboy, a Goth witch, and a suicidal man. Researching a mystery writing class for a college extension course, he undertook to put his experience, knowledge, and skills into a five-volume series laying out easy to understand and apply methods of writing a mystery. Beyond his fiction and non-fiction writing, he creates book covers and edits work for others. Catch more about him at http://www.authorrondvoigts.com.

Made in the USA
Monee, IL
17 March 2020